FRUIT/FRUTA

by/por Tea Benduhn

Reading consultant/Consultora de lectura: Susan Nations, M.Ed.,
author, literacy coach, consultant in literacy development/
autora, tutora de alfabetización, consultora de desarrollo de la lectura

WEEKLY READER®
PUBLISHING

Please visit our web site at: www.garethstevens.com
For a free color catalog describing our list of high-quality books,
call 1-800-542-2595 (USA) or 1-800-387-3178 (Canada).

Library of Congress Cataloging-in-Publication Data available upon request from publisher.

ISBN: 978-0-8368-8455-5 (lib. bdg.)
ISBN: 978-0-8368-8462-3 (softcover)

This edition first published in 2008 by
Weekly Reader® Books
An imprint of Gareth Stevens Publishing
1 Reader's Digest Road
Pleasantville, NY 10570-7000 USA

Copyright © 2008 by Gareth Stevens, Inc.

Managing editor: Valerie J. Weber
Art direction: Tammy West
Graphic designer: Scott Krall
Picture research: Diane Laska-Swanke
Photographer: Gregg Andersen
Production: Jessica Yanke
Spanish translation: Tatiana Acosta and Guillermo Gutiérrez

Printed in the United States of America

1 2 3 4 5 6 7 8 9 11 10 09 08 07

Note to Educators and Parents

Reading is such an exciting adventure for young children! They are beginning to integrate their oral language skills with written language. To encourage children along the path to early literacy, books must be colorful, engaging, and interesting; they should invite the young reader to explore both the print and the pictures.

The *Find Out About Food* series is designed to help children understand the value of good nutrition and eating to stay healthy. In each book, young readers will learn how their favorite foods — and possibly some new ones — fit into a balanced diet.

Each book is specially designed to support the young reader in the reading process. The familiar topics are appealing to young children and invite them to read — and re-read — again and again. The full-color photographs and enhanced text further support the student during the reading process.

In addition to serving as wonderful picture books in schools, libraries, homes, and other places where children learn to love reading, these books are specifically intended to be read within an instructional guided reading group. This small group setting allows beginning readers to work with a fluent adult model as they make meaning from the text. After children develop fluency with the text and content, the book can be read independently. Children and adults alike will find these books supportive, engaging, and fun!

— Susan Nations, M.Ed., author, literacy coach, and consultant in literacy development

Nota para los maestros y los padres

¡Leer es una aventura tan emocionante para los niños pequeños! A esta edad están comenzando a integrar su manejo del lenguaje oral con el lenguaje escrito. Para animar a los niños en el camino de la lectura incipiente, los libros deben ser coloridos, estimulantes e interesantes; deben invitar a los jóvenes lectores a explorar la letra impresa y las ilustraciones.

Conoce la comida es una colección diseñada para ayudar a los jóvenes lectores a entender la importancia de una nutrición apropiada y el papel de la alimentación en la salud. En cada libro, los jóvenes lectores aprenderán de qué forma sus alimentos favoritos —y posiblemente algunos nuevos— pueden formar parte de una dieta balanceada.

Cada libro está especialmente diseñado para ayudar a los jóvenes lectores en el proceso de lectura. Los temas familiares llaman la atención de los niños y los invitan a leer una y otra vez. Las fotografías a todo color y el tamaño de la letra ayudan aún más al estudiante en el proceso de lectura.

Además de servir como maravillosos libros ilustrados en escuelas, bibliotecas, hogares y otros lugares donde los niños aprenden a amar la lectura, estos libros han sido especialmente concebidos para ser leídos en un grupo de lectura guiada. Este contexto permite que los lectores incipientes trabajen con un adulto que domina la lectura mientras van determinando el significado del texto. Una vez que los niños dominan el texto y el contenido, el libro puede ser leído de manera independiente. ¡Estos libros les resultarán útiles, estimulantes y divertidos a niños y a adultos por igual!

— Susan Nations, M.Ed., autora, tutora de alfabetización, consultora de desarrollo de la lectura

Mom says I can have a treat. What will I pick? Strawberries, oranges, or bananas? I love all kinds of fruits.

Mamá dice que puedo comer algo rico. ¿Qué elegiré: fresas, naranjas o bananas? Toda la fruta me encanta.

Grape juice, applesauce, and
canned peaches are also fruits.
All of these fruits taste good.
Fruits are good for me, too.

El jugo de uva, la compota
de manzana y los melocotones
enlatados también son fruta.
Toda la fruta está rica. Además,
comer fruta me hace bien.

Fruits are part of the **food pyramid**.
The six colored bands on the food
pyramid stand for types of foods.
Make smart choices. Eat these
foods and **exercise** every day.

La fruta es parte de la **pirámide
alimentaria**. Cada una de las seis
franjas de colores de la pirámide
representa un tipo de alimento.
Elige de forma inteligente.
Consume estos alimentos y
haz **ejercicio** todos los días.

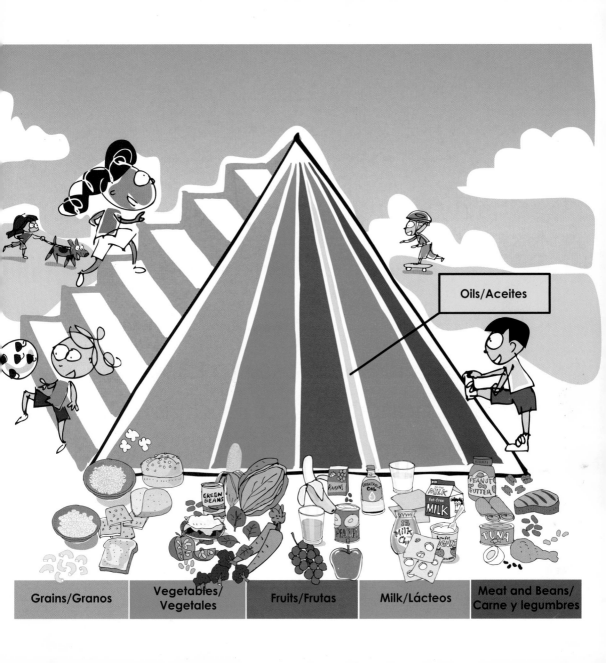

Oils/Aceites

Grains/Granos

Vegetables/
Vegetales

Fruits/Frutas

Milk/Lácteos

Meat and Beans/
Carne y legumbres

The red band stands for fruits. It is a wide band. You should eat lots of fruits every day.

La franja roja representa la fruta. Es una banda muy ancha. Debes comer mucha fruta todos los días.

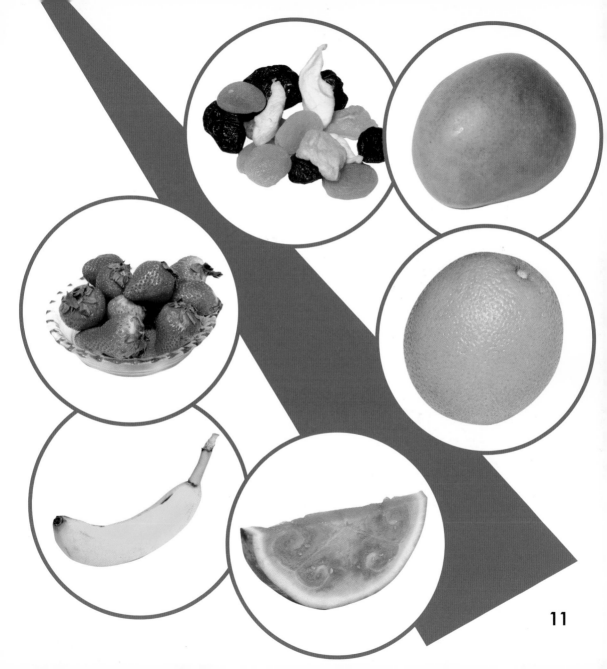

Eating fruit helps me stay **healthy**. Fruit is good for my heart. It helps my body heal cuts, too.

Comer fruta me ayuda a estar **saludable**. La fruta es buena para mi corazón. También ayuda a que mis heridas cicatricen rápido.

Eating fruit gives me **energy**. Bananas are good. I eat a banana before I play soccer.

Comer fruta me da **energía**. Las bananas son buenas. Siempre me como una banana antes de jugar al fútbol.

My family keeps a bowl of fruit on the kitchen table. I like peaches and plums. Sometimes I eat fruit salad for a snack.

En casa, siempre hay una fuente llena de fruta sobre la mesa de la cocina. Me gustan los melocotones y las ciruelas. A veces, meriendo una ensalada de frutas.

I bring dried fruit to school. I eat it with my lunch. Sometimes I have fresh fruit. I like crunchy apples and juicy oranges.

Llevo fruta deshidratada a la escuela. Me la como con el almuerzo. A veces, llevo fruta fresca. Me gustan las manzanas crujientes y las naranjas jugosas.

Do you help your parents shop for the fruits you like? I like to try new fruits. What will I try next?

¿Ayudas a tus padres a comprar la fruta que te gusta? A mí me gusta probar frutas nuevas. ¿Cuál será la próxima que voy a probar?

Glossary/Glosario

canned — sold or stored in a can with water, juice, or syrup added

energy — the strength and ability to be active

food pyramid — the drawing that shows six colored bands that stand for the six different food groups people should eat every day

healthy — strong and free from illness

soccer — a game played by two teams kicking a ball into one of two goals

----

energía — fuerza y capacidad de estar activo

enlatado — que se vende o conserva en latas con agua, jugo o almíbar

fútbol — juego en el que participan dos equipos que patean una pelota con la intención de anotar goles en la portería del equipo contrario

pirámide alimentaria — dibujo que muestra seis franjas de colores que representan seis grupos diferentes de alimentos que las personas deben comer a diario

saludable — fuerte y sin enfermedades

For More Information/Más información

Books/Libros

Fruits. Healthy Me (series). Jill Kalz (Smart Apple Media)

Fruits and Vegetables/Frutas y vegetales. English and Spanish Foundation (series). Gladys Rosa-Mendoza (me+mi publishing)

Las frutas. Los grupos de alimentos (series). Robin Nelson (Lerner Publications)

Web Sites/Páginas Web

My Pyramid for Kids
mypyramid.gov/kids/index.html
Click on links to play a game and learn more at the government's Web site about the food pyramid.

Index/Índice

About the Author/Información sobre la autora

Tea Benduhn writes and edits books for children and teens. She lives in the beautiful state of Wisconsin with her husband and two cats. The walls of their home are lined with bookshelves filled with books. Tea says, "I read every day. It is more fun than watching television!"

Tea Benduhn escribe y corrige libros para niños y adolescentes. Vive en el bello estado de Wisconsin con su esposo y dos gatos. Las paredes de su casa están cubiertas de estanterías con libros. Tea dice: "Leo todos los días. ¡Es más divertido que ver televisión!".